DUNHUANG

From the Neolithic Age to Today

Written by Zhao Xiaoxing
Illustrated by Zhao Peng
Translated by Li Chaoyuan

朝華出版社
BLOSSOM PRESS

Today, we're headed to Dunhuang. Come join us!

Dunhuang is home to the Mogao Caves, a world heritage that houses the most exquisite murals of ancient China.

It is the place to enjoy the beauty of Mingsha Mountain and the Crescent Spring. You can also take a camel ride in the desert.

Dunhuang produces the sweetest grapes, apricots, and honeydew melons around.

Once a fort of military strategic importance, Dunhuang was also a hub for East-West exchange along the ancient Silk Road.

It was truly a metropolis in ancient times.

As a gateway to the Western Regions, Dunhuang spanned a vast area including the Danghe River basin and the Shule River basin.

Human activities in Dunhuang date back to the Neolithic Age. Tools and crops from 1600 BC and ruins from 1000 BC were discovered there.

Ancient people used farming tools such as stone axes and adzes to grow crops like wheat and millet.

They made pottery into vessels, utensils, and even musical instruments. The vessel flute is known as the "xun."

They used stone arrowheads and other thin, portable tools for hunting wildlife including cattle, deer, Mongolian gazelles, and antelope.

According to records, Dunhuang began as a place where nomads settled and thrived. Nomadic tribes Wusun and Yuezhi once lived there.

Between the late Qin and early Han dynasties, the two tribes fought, and the Wusun chief was killed. The defeat forced the tribe to move north of the Tianshan Mountains.

乌孙人

月氏人

天山

月氏人

乌孙人

匈奴人

月氏人

In the start of the 2nd Century BC, the Xiongnu, another nomadic group, rose to power and defeated the Yuezhi to take control of the Hexi Corridor and the Western Regions.

The majority of the Yuezhi were then forced to migrate to the Ili River basin, which later became known as the Greater Yuezhi. Those who stayed in Dunhuang were known as the Lesser Yuezhi.

大月氏

伊犁河流域

In the early years of the Western Han Dynasty (202 BC - AD 8), the Xiongnu ruled over the Hexi Corridor and repeatedly invaded the northern border of the Han Dynasty, becoming a real threat to transportation and exchange between the Central Plains and Western Regions.

In 121 BC, Huo Qubing, a renowned military general of the Western Han Dynasty, launched two attacks against the Xiongnu and resumed Han control over the Hexi Corridor. Two prefectures, Wuwei and Jiuquan, were established in the region to strengthen Han's power.

In 139 BC, Han envoy Zhang Qian was dispatched to the Western Regions by Emperor Wu. Leading a convoy of 100 strong, Zhang was captured by the Xiongnu en route to the Hexi Corridor.

He never found a chance to escape until 129 BC. He continued westward, passing Ferghana and Sogdiana, before arriving in the land of Greater Yuezhi and then Bactria where he spent more than a year.

On his way back, Zhang was captured by the Xiongnu again. He managed to escape during Xiongnu unrest in 126 BC with his Xiongnu wife and assistant Ganfu. His expedition represented the first formal contact between the Central Plains and the Western Regions, and he was remembered as a pioneer for charting a course by later generations.

In 111 BC, Han introduced two new prefectures, Zhangye and Dunhuang, and built the Great Wall from Jiuquan to the west of Dunhuang. The Yumen Pass and Yangguan Pass were fortified to protect Dunhuang from invasion. Dunhuang thus became a military garrison outpost and the gateway to the Western Regions.

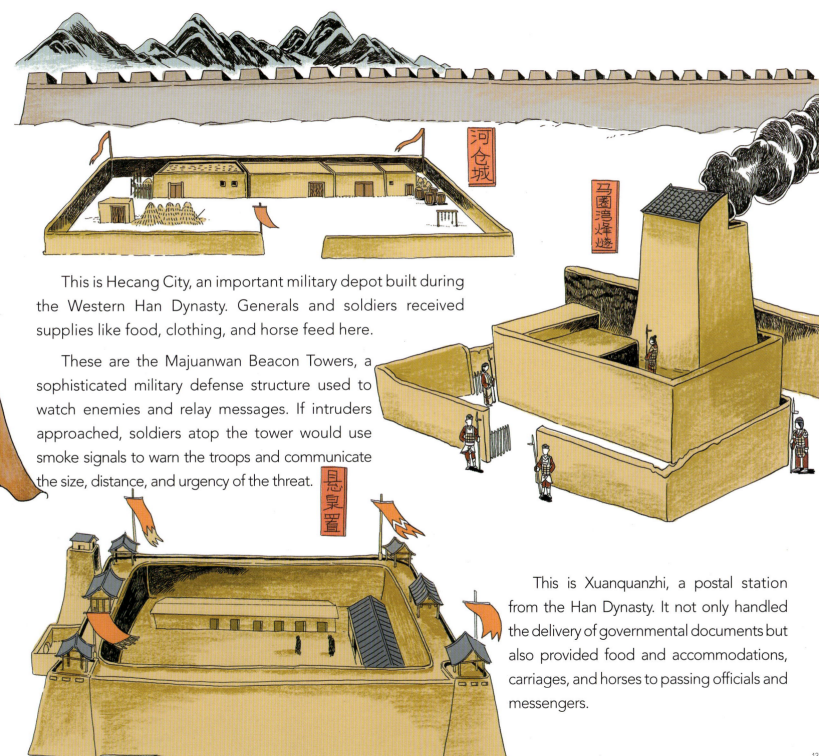

河仓城

马圈湾烽燧

This is Hecang City, an important military depot built during the Western Han Dynasty. Generals and soldiers received supplies like food, clothing, and horse feed here.

These are the Majuanwan Beacon Towers, a sophisticated military defense structure used to watch enemies and relay messages. If intruders approached, soldiers atop the tower would use smoke signals to warn the troops and communicate the size, distance, and urgency of the threat.

悬泉置

This is Xuanquanzhi, a postal station from the Han Dynasty. It not only handled the delivery of governmental documents but also provided food and accommodations, carriages, and horses to passing officials and messengers.

During the Western Han Dynasty, the Prefecture of Dunhuang had six counties under its jurisdiction: Dunhuang, Longle, Xiaogu, Guangzhi, Yuanquan, and Ming'an. All these names had special meanings.

"Dun" means grandness and "Huang" means prosperity, so "Dunhuang" means greatness and magnificence.

A story explains the name of Longle County. A herder in Dunhuang caught a flying horse with a bridle and presented it to Emperor Wu of the Han Dynasty. Believing the flying horse was from Heaven, he thought it should be in the possession of the emperor. The place where the creature was reportedly caught was named Longle, with "long" meaning "dragon" (referring to the name of the horse breed) and "le" meaning the bridle.

Xiaogu County used to be called Yuzezhang. During the Han Dynasty, its mayor Cui Buyi taught people how to farm and encouraged them to work with diligence ("xiao") so that they would harvest abundant grains ("gu"). The county was named to honor the mayor and the virtue.

Yuanquan County was named for the many ("yuan") springs ("quan") in the area. This speaks volumes on the climate of Dunhuang in the past: It was not as dry as it is now.

Emperor Wu of the Western Han Dynasty relocated residents from inland to Dunhuang several times and mobilized them and soldiers to prepare more land for agriculture. At that point, Dunhuang started gradually becoming an important hub for transportation and trade between the inland and the Western Regions.

In 9, Wang Mang usurped the throne and brought the Western Han Dynasty to an end, throwing the Central Plains into chaos. Dunhuang and other parts of Hexi also became vulnerable. Dou Rong, a respected official in the capital, volunteered to serve in Gansu. Due to his contributions to national unity and public welfare, Dou was appointed General-in-Chief of Hexi and managed the affairs of the five prefectures.[1]

①In addition to the four prefectures (Wuwei, Zhangye, Jiuquan, and Dunhuang) in Hexi, Jincheng (today's Lanzhou) was established as a prefecture during the reign of the Emperor Zhao of the Han Dynasty, making a total of Five Prefectures in Hexi.

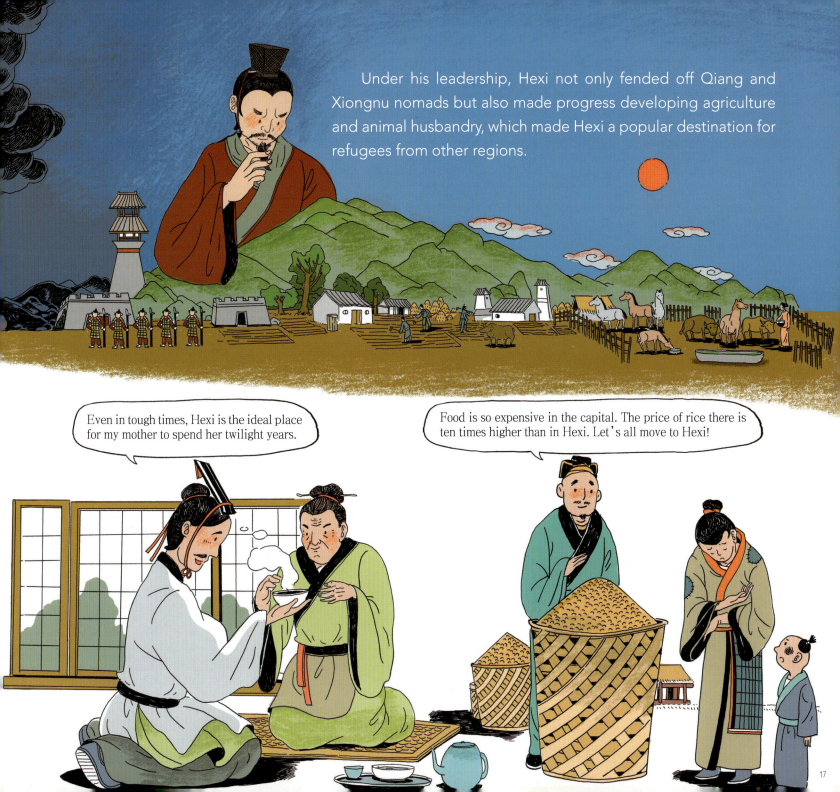

Under his leadership, Hexi not only fended off Qiang and Xiongnu nomads but also made progress developing agriculture and animal husbandry, which made Hexi a popular destination for refugees from other regions.

Even in tough times, Hexi is the ideal place for my mother to spend her twilight years.

Food is so expensive in the capital. The price of rice there is ten times higher than in Hexi. Let's all move to Hexi!

During the Eastern Han Dynasty (25-220), Han authorities made Dunhuang the military center for exercising control over the Western Regions to hedge against the increasing power of the northern Xiongnu nomads.

In 137, the northern Xiongnu nomads invaded the Western Regions. Pei Cen, then mayor of Dunhuang, led 3,000 soldiers to fight the enemies in the Western Regions and returned victorious.

A stele was erected to commemorate this triumph.

文 武
双 全

张芝墨池

Zhang Huan was another famous general who won battles against Xiongnu nomads in Dunhuang. He was also a renowned scholar.

His son Zhang Zhi became a famous calligrapher known as the Sage of Cursive Script. Reportedly, Zhang Zhi was so diligent at his craft that the pond beside which he often practiced calligraphy was dyed black from brush washing so many times.

In that era, a place in Dunhuang was named Xiaofutuli, meaning "minor Buddhist alley." The name might indicate that Buddhism had been introduced to Dunhuang.

Cao Pi, Emperor Wen of Wei of the Three Kingdoms period, inherited and maintained the policy of military settlement, which greatly boosted economic growth in Dunhuang. In 227, Cang Ci was appointed mayor of Dunhuang.

He cracked down on the power of rich landlords and sought to maintain equity in society. He took many measures to foster peace and prosperity in Dunhuang.

Land should be redistributed so that all peasants could own their own land.

Pending disputes should be resolved in a just and swift manner.

Foreign merchants should be protected from blackmail and fraud. Soldiers should be dispatched to protect passing caravans when necessary.

In 249, Huangfu Long became mayor of Dunhuang. He vigorously popularized effective farming tools and techniques from the Central Plains, which contributed to increased yields of local crops. He also introduced new styles of women's clothes.

With these new tools and techniques, yields increased by 50% while requiring only half the labor.

With this seed drill, sowing became so efficient!

This new skirt is both comfortable and affordable. It doesn't require much cloth.

In the early years of the Western Jin Dynasty, Wu Yan, former general of the Wu Kingdom, was appointed mayor of Dunhuang. Dunhuang experienced continued economic prosperity thanks to his emphasis on agricultural development.

Dharmaraksa, a Buddhist monk since the age of eight, traveled extensively throughout the Western Regions and spoke multiple languages. During the reign of Emperor Wu of the Jin Dynasty, he brought many Buddhist scriptures from Dunhuang to Chang'an. He was committed to translating them and spreading the teachings to people along the way.

Dharmaraksa returned to Dunhuang in 284. Throughout his life, he translated 165 Buddhist scriptures, winning the title "Bodhisattva of Dunhuang."

敦煌太守

吾彦

竺法护

The highly developed culture in Dunhuang nourished many eminent scholars.

敦煌五龙

Suo Jing, Fan Zhong, Zhang Han, Suo Zhen, and Suo Yong, who all attended the imperial academy together, were collectively known as the "Five Masters of Dunhuang."

After visiting Mingsha Mountain, he inscribed the three characters for "Xian Yan Temple" (now defunct) on a cliff near Mogao Caves.

仙巖寺

Suo Jing was from Longle County. He was a famous general, scholar, and calligraphy theorist in the Western Jin Dynasty. He was a master of cursive script and authored *the Treatise on Cursive Script*.

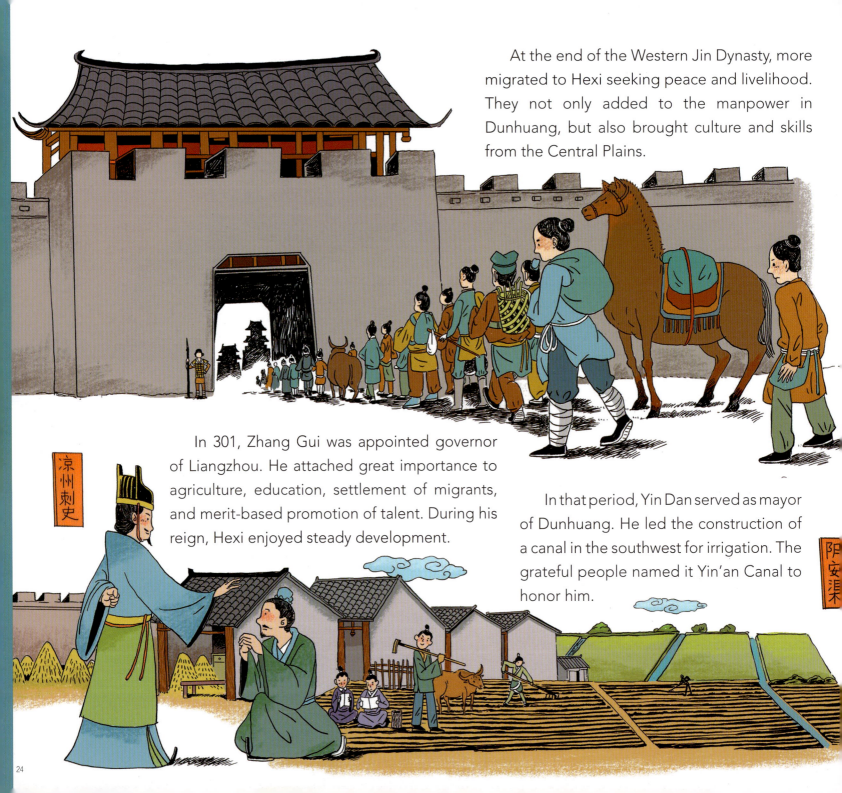

At the end of the Western Jin Dynasty, more migrated to Hexi seeking peace and livelihood. They not only added to the manpower in Dunhuang, but also brought culture and skills from the Central Plains.

凉州刺史

In 301, Zhang Gui was appointed governor of Liangzhou. He attached great importance to agriculture, education, settlement of migrants, and merit-based promotion of talent. During his reign, Hexi enjoyed steady development.

In that period, Yin Dan served as mayor of Dunhuang. He led the construction of a canal in the southwest for irrigation. The grateful people named it Yin'an Canal to honor him.

阳安渠

In 345, Zhang Jun, governor of Liangzhou, established the prefecture of Shazhou by merging the three prefectures of Dunhuang, Jinchang, and Gaochang with three military camps, with Dunhuang as its administrative centre. Yang Xuan was appointed governor of Shazhou. During his reign, he advocated building water conservancy projects and irrigation systems including reconstructing the Ping Canal to the Yangkai Canal.

Painting the walls of tombs was popular in Dunhuang at that time. Common patterns involved legendary birds and animals as well as real-life scenes such as farming, harvesting, grazing, cooking, and feasting.

In 366, a monk named Yue Zun was meditating at the cliff of Mingsha Mountain and suddenly saw thousands of golden rays shining like thousands of Buddha images. He was thus inspired to build the first of the Mogao Caves.

鸣沙山

乐僔

In 376, Former Qin officials conquered the Former Liang and brought the Hexi region, including Dunhuang, under its jurisdiction. Emperor Fu Jian relocated more than 17,000 households from the Jianghan region and the Central Plains to Dunhuang, which boosted local development.

General Lü Guang of the Former Qin brought back renowned translator and eminent monk Kumarajiva from Qiuci. During the journey, Kumarajiva's white horse died in Dunhuang. The White Horse Pagoda located in the west of Dunhuang was reportedly built in memory of it.

鸠摩罗什

Last night in a dream, my horse told me he was sent by Buddha to escort me to Chang'an to spread Buddhist teachings. Now that the mission is accomplished, he said it was time for him to leave.

Meng Min, mayor of Dunhuang during the Later Liang Dynasty, won great respect from the people for constructing an irrigation canal in southern Dunhuang. People named it Menshou Canal after him and raised a temple in his name.

After Fu Jian died, Lü Guang took control of Liangzhou and established the Later Liang Dynasty. In 395, social unrest in Later Liang forced thousands of households to move to Dunhuang.

挤 挤 挤

孟敏

敦煌

孟庙

孟授渠

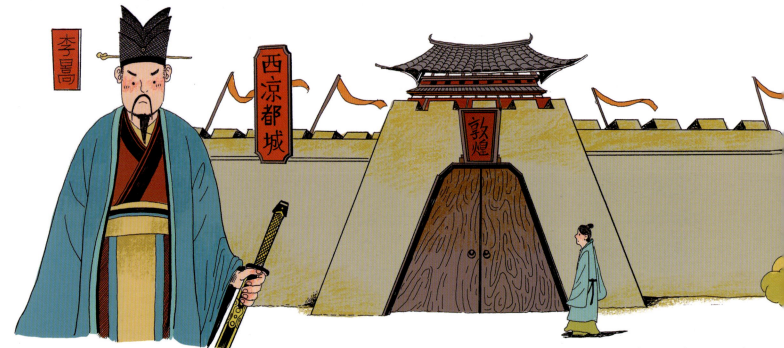

In 400, Li Hao, then mayor of Dunhuang, was appointed Grand General and Duke of Liang. He established the Western Liang regime and set its capital in Dunhuang. It was the first time Dunhuang served as a capital.

Western Liang established a three-tiered administrative system consisting of counties, towns, and neighborhoods.

Dunhuang enjoyed good harvests and prosperity thanks to proagriculture policies.

Li Hao built a temple to honor his father and established the official educational institution known as the Pan Palace which enrolled up to 500 students. Kingdoms from the Western Regions such as Khotan (Yutian) and Shanshan began to pay tributes to Dunhuang.

The Northern Liang regime, established by nomad leader Juqu Mengxun, began posing a significant threat to Western Liang. Li consequently relocated the capital to Jiuquan in 405. He also relocated 23,000 households, which greatly undermined the strength of Dunhuang.

Dunhuang is famous for its diligent and talented people. My son, you must implement policies that benefit the people.

After moving its capital to Jiuquan, Western Liang reinforced the defense of Dunhuang by restoring several sections of obsolete forts and walls.

In 420, Northern Liang defeated Western Liang. The Northern Liang authorities appointed Suo Yuanxu mayor of Dunhuang. However, he was disliked by many for being militant. Officials Song Cheng and Zhang Hong joined former mayor Li Xun to expel him from Dunhuang.

Li Xun was appointed governor of Liangzhou. When Juqu Mengxun sent troops to attack Dunhuang, Li held back on retaliation to strengthen his defenses. In 421, the overwhelming might of the enemy troops brought defeat to Li Xun, who ended up committing suicide. It was a heavy blow to Dunhuang.

Though of Xiongnu ancestry, Juqu Mengxun placed great emphasis on Han culture and acquainted himself with scholars from Dunhuang. Figures such as Kan Yin, Song Yao, and Liu Bing were all granted important positions. Liu Bing was honored as Grand Preceptor.

People of different ethnic groups should unite as one.

The Northern Liang regime built the first three caves (Caves 268, 272 and 275) of the Mogao Caves. They were multifunctional chambers for meditation, sermons, and rituals.

275

268

In 439, the Northern Liang was conquered by the Northern Wei regime. Juqu Wuhui, mayor of Jiuquan under Northern Liang, fled to Dunhuang to continue to resist Northern Wei. Three years later, he abandoned Dunhuang and took 10,000 households with him. They were the backbone of the Hexi region. Dunhuang suffered another heavy blow.

In 442, Li Bao, grandson of Li Hao, occupied Dunhuang and pledged allegiance to the Northern Wei regime. He was appointed governor of Shazhou and Duke of Dunhuang. During his reign, he restored the city and settled migrants. Dunhuang was able to recover.

In 444, to better manage the Western Regions and defend against the Rouran Kingdom, the Northern Wei regime asserted direct control over Dunhuang and revitalized the Silk Road. Again, the route was bustling with caravans.

固若金汤

Not long after, Rouran gained control over the Western Regions. Thanks to the sweat and toil of generals, soldiers, and civilians, Dunhuang survived the war.

In 485, Mu Liang was appointed grand general of Dunhuang. His generous policies contributed to the recovery of Dunhuang's economy. However, quick recovery of manpower and resources was difficult after years of warfare caused a substantial loss of population.

In 524, Dunhuang was renamed Guazhou ("Melon Prefecture") because it produced exceptionally sweet fruits due to a wide difference between day and night temperatures. The Northern Wei regime appointed imperial clan member Yuan Rong governor of Guazhou. He remained in the office for nearly two decades. Yuan not only maintained stability and developed the economy, but sponsored copying of Buddhist sutras and construction of large parts of the Mogao Caves.

Murals produced in this period featured various stories and narratives. The most famous piece was the Nine-Colored Deer series, *Jataka of Deer King*, in Cave 257.

The famous Cave 285 (known as the "Cave of Prince Dongyang") was also built during Yuan's reign. The murals in this period showcased a new aesthetic style, probably introduced by Yuan from the Central Plains, characterized by slim and handsome figures in loose gowns with wide girdles.

Look how thin this person is! And his loose clothes look so elegant! This must be the fashion of the Central Plains!

Early Dunhuang murals portrayed figures as stout and robust, influenced by the style of the Western Regions.

During the early years of the Northern Zhou Dynasty (577-581), Linghu Xiu served as mayor of Dunhuang. People had great respect for his integrity and frugality. During his reign, Dunhuang enjoyed stability and prosperity, which also facilitated trade and contact between the Central Plains and the Western Regions.

Yu Yi continued his predecessor's efforts to build caves and statues during his tenure as governor of Guazhou. Cave 428 is believed to have been built and funded under his leadership, with contributions from over 1,000 monks and commoners from Shazhou and Liangzhou.

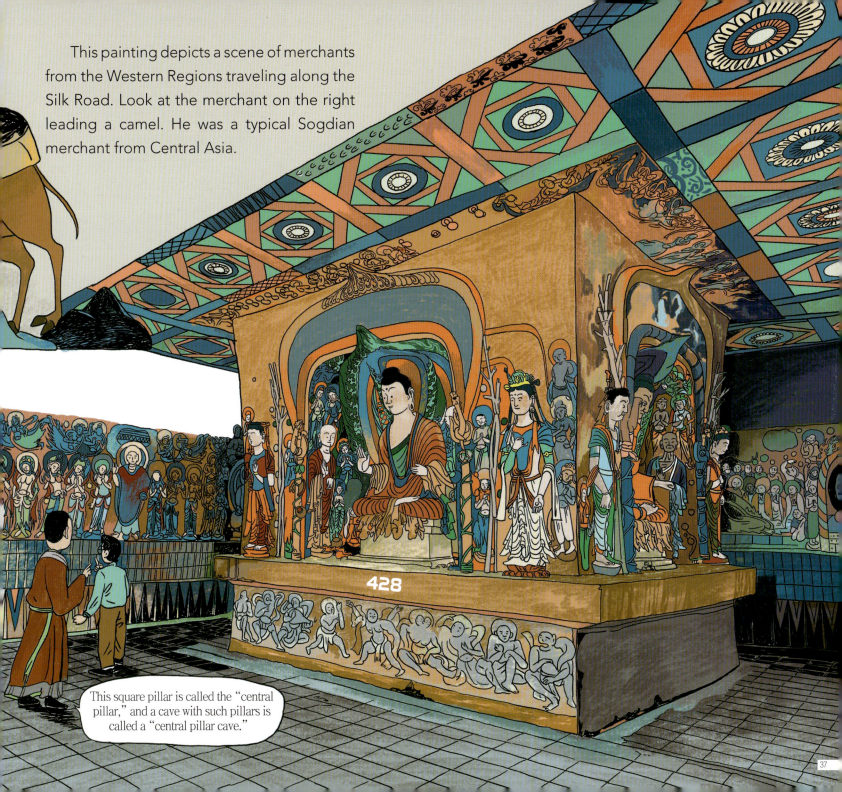

This painting depicts a scene of merchants from the Western Regions traveling along the Silk Road. Look at the merchant on the right leading a camel. He was a typical Sogdian merchant from Central Asia.

428

This square pillar is called the "central pillar," and a cave with such pillars is called a "central pillar cave."

The Sui Dynasty reunited the Chinese nation. In 607, Guazhou was renamed Dunhuang Prefecture. However, during this time, Zhangye became a more popular destination for merchants from the Western Regions.

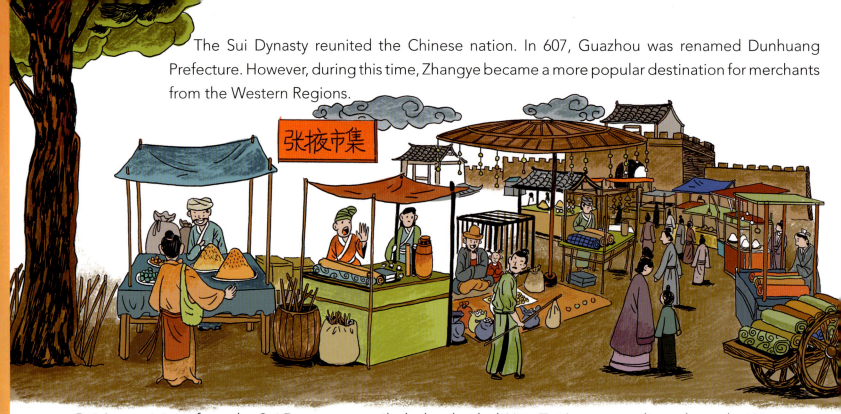

Pei Ju, a minister from the Sui Dynasty, compiled a book titled *Xiyu Tuji* (a compendium about the Western Regions) based on information collected while managing trade markets in Zhangye. The book detailed the geography, surnames, customs, clothing, and products of 44 kingdoms. Maps were also included.

During the Sui Dynasty, three routes connected the Western Regions: the northern branch of the ancient Silk Road, the central branch, and the southern branch. These routes converged at Dunhuang. This made Dunhuang the most crucial crux of the Silk Road.

Between 605 and 616, envoys from over 30 kingdoms in the Western Regions began to pay tributes to the Sui Dynasty, presenting a wealth of their specialties. Sui envoys also brought various goods from the Western Regions to Chang'an. Increasing exchange between the Central Plains and the Western Regions helped Dunhuang regain its status as a hub for economic and cultural interaction.

Gaochang Kingdom presented cinnabar salt and wine as tributes, Kangju offered Asana and other spices, Qiuci contributed Benzoin and fine steeds, Yutian brought exquisite jade, and the Tocharians presented celestial stallions.

I brought back five-colored salt from An, agate from Jinbin (Kophen), and dancers from Shi Kingdom.

Emperors of the Sui Dynasty embraced Buddhism. Emperor Wen issued a decree requiring every prefecture to build a stūpa to preserve the relics of Buddha. Dunhuang built a stūpa in Chongjiao Monastery, situated within the Mogao Caves.

Many caves in Mogao were built during the Sui Dynasty. Buddhist scriptures copied by the Sui imperial family were found in the Library Cave (Cave 17).

In the Library Cave is *the Siyi Sūtra* copied by Princess Cui, consort of Prince Qin (Yang Jun) of Sui. Also housed there were *the Daloutan Sūtra* and *Sūtra of Prince Mupo*, both penned by Empress Dugu of Sui, as well as *the Mahaparanirvana Sūtra* by Emperor Yang of Sui when he was a prince.

427

With advanced textile and dyeing technologies, the Sui Dynasty produced fine silk with exquisite patterns. Input and influence from the Western Regions reached the Central Plains and greatly enriched the patterns and styles of Sui textiles.

This cave has very big Buddha statues!

The Lian Zhu Wen ("connecting beads pattern") was a typical decoration on Persian brocade during the Sui Dynasty. It featured a series of interconnected circles adorned with images of phoenixes, tigers, lions, elephants, horses, and flowers resulting in a vibrant and lively design. These patterns soon became popular in the Central Plains.

Towards the end of the Sui Dynasty and in the early years of the Tang Dynasty, Dunhuang was far from peaceful and grappled with threats from internal separatists and external invaders.

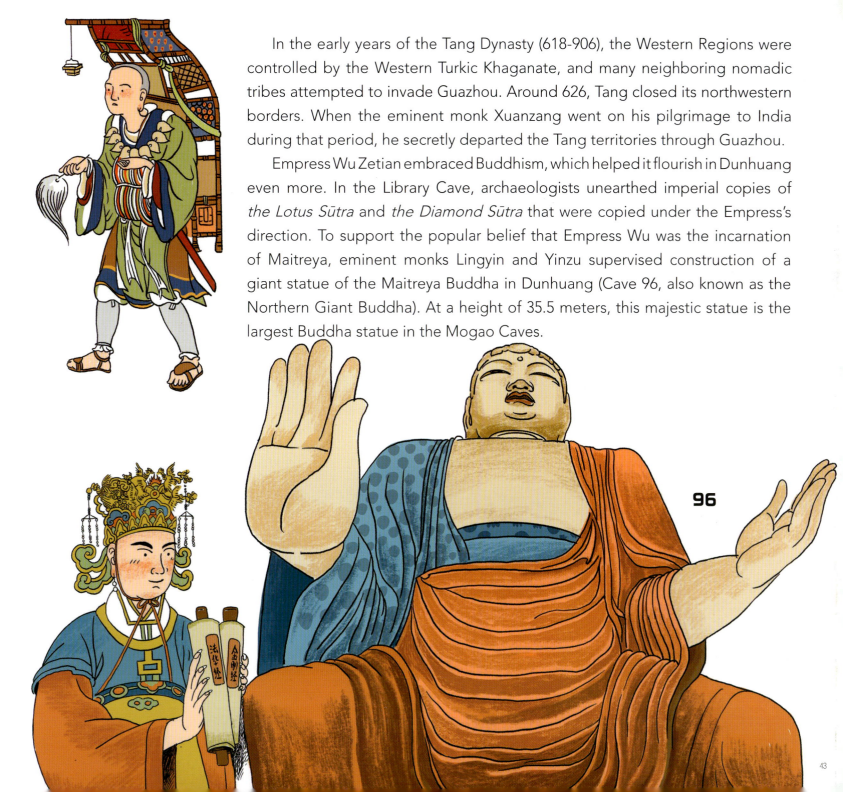

In the early years of the Tang Dynasty (618-906), the Western Regions were controlled by the Western Turkic Khaganate, and many neighboring nomadic tribes attempted to invade Guazhou. Around 626, Tang closed its northwestern borders. When the eminent monk Xuanzang went on his pilgrimage to India during that period, he secretly departed the Tang territories through Guazhou.

Empress Wu Zetian embraced Buddhism, which helped it flourish in Dunhuang even more. In the Library Cave, archaeologists unearthed imperial copies of *the Lotus Sūtra* and *the Diamond Sūtra* that were copied under the Empress's direction. To support the popular belief that Empress Wu was the incarnation of Maitreya, eminent monks Lingyin and Yinzu supervised construction of a giant statue of the Maitreya Buddha in Dunhuang (Cave 96, also known as the Northern Giant Buddha). At a height of 35.5 meters, this majestic statue is the largest Buddha statue in the Mogao Caves.

96

With Han culture from the Central Plains spreading westward, Buddhist art in the Mogao Caves reached a new era. The murals in Cave 220 depicted not only scenes of Buddhist temples in Chang'an, but also images of Tang emperors and leaders and envoys from various kingdoms. The glory of the Tang Dynasty during the Zhenguan period (626-649) was captured in the Mogao Caves.

220

The Tang Dynasty witnessed extensive exchange and fusion of music and arts between the Central Plains and the Western Regions. Dances from the Western Regions became popular both in the imperial court and among the commoners. The four dancers depicted at the bottom of the mural are dancing in pairs. The joyful style originated in the Western Regions.

The elderly man seated here is Vimalakirti, who is well-versed in Mahayana Buddhism and immensely wealthy. He is debating Manjushri Bodhisattva, the wisest figure in Buddhism. The renowned Tang poet Wang Wei, drawing inspiration from Vimalakirti (pronounced Weimojie in Chinese), adopted the courtesy name Mojie.

维摩诘

文殊

So many people have come to watch the debate! Look at the Tang emperor! He wears a crown with tassels and a robe adorned with sun and moon symbols reserved solely for emperors.

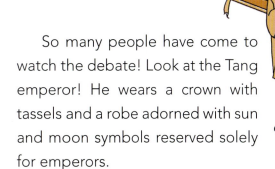

These are leaders and envoys from various kingdoms. The man in the tall hat and brocade robe is a Persian prince, and the one with two feathers on his hat is from Korea. The Tang Dynasty had close relations with many kingdoms.

During the glorious years of Tang, Dunhuang was able to continue developing thanks to growing national strength despite frequent tension coming from the northwest. The Tang regime effectively managed the Dunhuang region with a well-organized system.

Suo Licai, age 15, resides in Xiaogu with his widowed mother, age 56. We have finished calculating how much land this household should get.

From the reign of Emperor Gaozong of Tang through Empress Wu to Emperor Xuanzong, extensive land reclamation was carried out in the Hexi region, leading to significant agricultural development in Dunhuang. The irrigation system improved significantly, with Dunhuang County alone boasting six main canals and 116 branch canals, forming a robust network of irrigation.

A stringent water management and allocation system was designed to manage water resources.

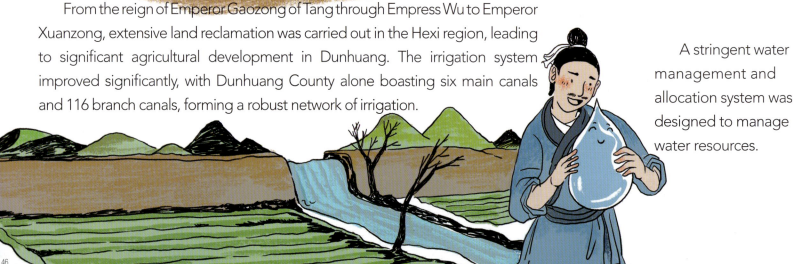

46

In those days, marketplaces in Dunhuang were filled with all kinds of goods: silk and porcelain from the Central Plains, jade and jewelry from the Western Regions, textiles, camels, and horses from the north, and local grains. Envoys, merchants, monks, and commoners passed back and forth through Dunhuang while traveling between the Central Plains and the Western Regions, as well as between India, West Asia, and China.

The Mogao Caves flourished during this period. With more than 1,000 shrines, it was a spectacular site. Dunhuang art and Tang style from the Central Plains enjoyed perfect fusion. Painted sculpture excelled in detailing their style. The blissful Buddhist land portrayed in the murals reflected the reality of the mundane world at that time.

This is the most exquisite and complete set of statues in Dunhuang. You can see the Buddha seated in the middle, with two disciples beside him, followed by two graceful Bodhisattvas and two heavenly kings at the outermost.

45

217

45

These merchants are from Sogdiana. They encounter robbers on their way. Look, they have a bundle of silk. Everyone loved Chinese silk back then.

The peasants are working in the fields despite the rain. Here's a lovely family enjoying dinner together.

23

After the outbreak of the An Shi Rebellion in 755, the Tang Dynasty dispatched elite troops from the northwest to the Central Plains. Tibet took advantage of the situation and occupied many areas in Longyou and Hexi regions.

In 786, Shazhou made an alliance with Tibet with the condition of retaining the population in Dunhuang. Dunhuang therefore came under the jurisdiction of Tibet.

The Tibetan rulers implemented assimilation policies like requiring the Han people to wear Tibetan costumes and speak the Tibetan language. The policies provoked resentment among people in Dunhuang and even resulted in social unrest.

The authorities noticed the problem and turned to privileged families for help to ease ethnic conflicts. They also vigorously supported Buddhism to improve social cohesion.

As a result, Buddhism flourished in Dunhuang. Monasteries increased from 13 to 17. Many monks were Tang officials and nobles unwilling to cooperate with the Tibetan regime. They helped improve the literacy of the monks and played an important role in maintaining stability in Dunhuang.

I am a decent official of Tang. I can't accept the Tibetan regime. I'd rather be a monk.

In Tibet, monks can participate in political affairs and serve as the Tsenpo's consultants.

Mahayana, an eminent monk from Dunhuang, even spread Zen Buddhist teachings at the Tibetan court, which incited a debate on whether monks can have epiphany or if they must be enlightened gradually. The debate was called the Tibetan Monks' Criticism Conference.

People must be enlightened gradually.

莲花戒

Epiphany!

摩诃衍

In 848, Zhang Yichao, a native of Dunhuang, seized opportunity brought by social unrest in Tibet and led a revolt against the regime. Zhang successfully recovered Guazhou and Shazhou for Tang. Later, they also reclaimed Suzhou, Ganzhou, and Yizhou.

In 851, he sent his brother Zhang Yitan to the Tang capital of Chang'an with a map and census record of the 11 prefectures in Hexi and Longyou regions to report on the victory to the Tang emperor.

Indeed Guanxi is a cradle of the best generals.

In the same year, the Tang Dynasty appointed Zhang Yichao head of the Guiyi Army, and Dunhuang officially entered the Guiyi Army period. In October 866, the army managed a vast stretch of land with six prefectures and a population of one million under its jurisdiction.

In 867, Zhang Yichao moved to Chang'an for his final years to demonstrate his faithfulness to Tang. Considerable competition accompanied the selection of his successor. After much fighting between Zhang, Suo, Li, and other influential families, Zhang Chengfeng secured the position. By then, the Guiyi Army only held Guazhou and Shazhou under its jurisdiction.

After learning of the fall of the Tang Dynasty in 909, Zhang Chengfeng proclaimed himself "Son of Heaven in White" and established the Western Han Jinshan Kingdom. "Western Han" means the kingdom of the Han people in the west, while "Jinshan" refers to the Golden Saddle Mountain in Dunhuang.

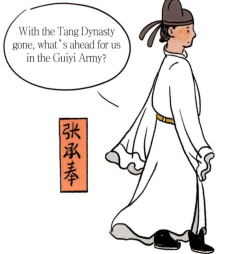

> With the Tang Dynasty gone, what's ahead for us in the Guiyi Army?

> I heard the *White Bird Song* is popular among the people. The white bird is an auspicious sign – considering founding your own kingdom and becoming king.

The Jinshan Kingdom aspired to recover their lost land but continued losing wars. In 911, when the Huihu (an ancient minority ethnic group) attacked, Jinshan was forced into an alliance with Huihu because Jinshan was so weak after years of war. The alliance required the Jinshan king to consider himself son of the Huihu Khan.

In 914, Cao Yijin, from another big family in Dunhuang, replaced Zhang Chengfeng. Cao believed he needed the power of the Central Plains to secure peace, so he honored the Central Plains authorities in orthodox ways.

Cao exercised matrimonial diplomacy by marrying his two daughters to the Ganzhou Huihu Khan and King of Khotan, respectively. Meanwhile, he gained considerable support from the people by absorbing members of prestigious families and leaders of minority ethnic groups into Guiyi Army leadership.

The Guiyi Army recovered considerable strength. Dunhuang remained an important hub on the Silk Road, and the markets were still teeming with various goods from different places.

We sell all kinds of spices and clothes. You will find walnuts, gardenias, galangal, haritaki, betel nuts, dill, pepper, fructus ulmi, rheum officinale, sesame oil, garlic, lotus roots, sweet dried dates, pomegranate, alum, comfrey, radix lithospermi, granulated sugar, maltose, coats, robes, wide leg pants, shoes, silk hats and scarves, waistbands, and other accessories. We also have incense sticks!

After Cao Yijin, the Cao family remained in control of the Guiyi Army regime in Dunhuang. Cao Yuanzhong, the third son of Cao Yijin, led it the longest. He brought stability and prosperity to Dunhuang by maintaining good relationships with neighbouring ethnic groups and the capital in the Central Plains.

A pious Buddhist, he founded an official Buddhist painting academy and built large caves. During his reign, the Manjusri Temple (Cave 61) was built and the Northern Giant Buddha statue (Cave 96) was repaired.

I'd like to thank the workers by cooking them a meal.

Thank you, my love. They worked really hard to repair the wooden structure in the lower part of the giant statue.

When a famous Indian monk and his disciples were passing through Dunhuang, Dunhuang official Cao Yanlu detained them for several months and requested they preach the Dharma in the region.

After Cao Yuanzhong, the Guiyi Army regime in Dunhuang fell into decline and began grappling with many threats. In the early 11th Century, the people in Dunhuang placed many sutras, paintings, and other cultural artifacts into a cave, sealed the door, and painted murals over it to conceal them. When the door was discovered by later generations, it became known as the Library Cave.

409

The Guiyi Army regime was replaced by the nomadic regime of Shazhou Huihu in 1030. It should not come as a surprise that some caves painted in this period feature images of nomadic khans in dragon robes.

In 1036, the Tangut began occupying Dunhuang. Two years later, Tangut established the Xixia regime, which mostly waged war with the Song and Liao regimes and exercised little control over Dunhuang. Many considered Dunhuang still under the jurisdiction of Shazhou Huihu.

Envoys!

From 1023 to 1050, the Shazhou regime paid tributes to the Northern Song Dynasty seven times.

In 1038, Li Yuanhao of the Tangut claimed the throne and established the Xixia Kingdom. Around 1068, Xixia strengthened its direct control over Guazhou and Shazhou.
The Yulin Caves were mainly built during the Xixia period.

This is a sacred Buddhist site. My family is the patron of this cave. Painting an image of the most revered Tangut monk on the wall will ensure my family is blessed.

29

In 1082, many were recruited by Xixia from Guazhou and Shazhou to fight the Northern Song Dynasty. In 1110, a famine swept across Guazhou, Shazhou, and Suzhou, forcing many to flee to other places. Dunhuang was heavily impacted.

Because of Xixia's control, many merchants from the Western Regions chose to bypass Dunhuang and reach the Central Plains via Qinghai or Mongolia. Dunhuang gradually lost its vital status on the Silk Road.

Faithful Buddhists, Xixia leaders absorbed diverse Buddhist cultural elements from the neighbouring regions, so the caves during this period were innovative with a range of artistic styles. Tibetan Tantric Buddhism was also introduced to Xixia, and the first Tibetan Tantric Cave was built in the Mogao Caves.

465

In 1227, the Mongols conquered the Xixia and occupied Dunhuang, placing it under the fiefdom of Batu, grandson of Genghis Khan. In 1277, Kublai Khan, Emperor of the Yuan Dynasty, took Dunhuang back under the direct jurisdiction of the central government.

Dunhuang again became an important hub along the Hexi route. Shortly after the establishment of the Yuan Dynasty, Marco Polo traveled to Dunhuang.

The people were mostly engaged in farming, and wheat was their major crop. The city's many monasteries held various Buddha statues. For funerals, a diviner would be invited to determine the date, and offerings like paper figures and horses were prepared for the deceased.

In 1280, Shazhou was upgraded to a higher administrative level. In 1292, the Yuan Dynasty forced people to migrate from Shazhou and Guazhou to Ganzhou. This policy made Guazhou and Shazhou nearly abandoned for a while.

Emperor Chengzong of Yuan later sent troops back to Guazhou and Shazhou to guard the region. The Yuan Dynasty maintained control over Dunhuang by appointing royal clan members as governors and leveraging the influence of Buddhism.

The family of King of Xining (Sulaiman) governing Shazhou built a stele inscribed with a six-syllabled Sanskrit mantra in the Mogao Caves. His successor rebuilt the Huangqing Temple in the Mogao Caves.

In 1368, the Ming Dynasty was established. In 1372, General Feng Sheng built Jiayuguan Pass to guard the western frontiers of Ming. The Jiayuguan-Hami route became a popular passage connecting the Central Plains and the Western Regions while Dunhuang was abandoned.

The Ming Dynasty indirectly managed Dunhuang by appointing descendants of the Mongols as governors and establishing seven garrisons as a buffer zone to fend off invaders from the west.

In 1404, the Shazhou Garrison was established in Dunhuang. In 1479, the Handong Garrison was established in the Dunhuang region. The Ming Dynasty was busy managing internal and external threats and did not make much progress in cultural development in Dunhuang. No new caves were built in Mogao.

In 1516, Dunhuang was occupied by Turpan nobilities. Dunhuang's population dwindled and many retreated inland. Worse still, its cultural heritage was almost lost. Without maintenance, many lower chambers in the Mogao Caves were buried in the sand, and the Buddha statues were damaged.

In 1644, the Qing Dynasty replaced the Ming. During the reign of Emperor Kangxi, the Qing Dynasty revitalized vast areas west of Jiayuguan Pass. In 1723, Dunhuang became an administrative region, later upgraded to Shazhou Garrison.

Upon the suggestion of General Yue Zhongqi, the Qing government relocated over 2,400 households to Dunhuang and provided each household with land, working animals, farming tools, seeds, and food to help them survive and thrive in the new place.

In 1727, Wang Long was sent by the Qing court to Dunhuang to supervise construction of a new city, government offices, and barracks.

In 1760, Shazhou Garrison was upgraded to Dunhuang County. Thanks to progress in irrigation and farming, Dunhuang's economy and population grew rapidly. The Mogao Caves once again became a sacred place for Buddhists.

Between 1796 and 1850, Buddhists in Dunhuang carried out extensive restoration and renovation of the Mogao Caves, but artistically little was improved.

344

Come pray in front of Guanyin Bodhisattva! She will ensure we have a baby next year!

Between 1862 and 1875, amid uprisings in northwestern China, Dunhuang became a battlefield and suffered population decline and economic losses.

At the end of the 19th Century, a Taoist named Wang Yuanlu arrived at the Mogao Caves.

Wang then became the self-proclaimed abbot of the Mogao Caves and used the offerings collected to repair the caves at his will. In 1900, he accidentally discovered the Library Cave while clearing accumulated sand.

Initially, Wang gave away some scripture scrolls, Buddhist paintings, and other items to local officials and gentry as gifts, but the recipients had no idea about their value. In 1904, the governor of Gansu ordered Wang Zonghan, the mayor of Dunhuang, to seal up the Library Cave and entrusted Abbot Wang to safeguard it and prevent its contents from being taken away.

The Library Cave was one of the most important archaeological discoveries of the early 20th Century. It contains about 70,000 ancient manuscripts of various kinds including not only many Buddhist scriptures, but also valuable official and private manuscripts and materials in minority ethnic languages.

The art in the Library Cave also holds silk paintings, hemp fabric paintings, paper paintings, silk banners, embroidery, and wooden sculpture. The manuscripts and artifacts are invaluable as a rich encyclopedia of firsthand evidence of how ancient human society functioned.

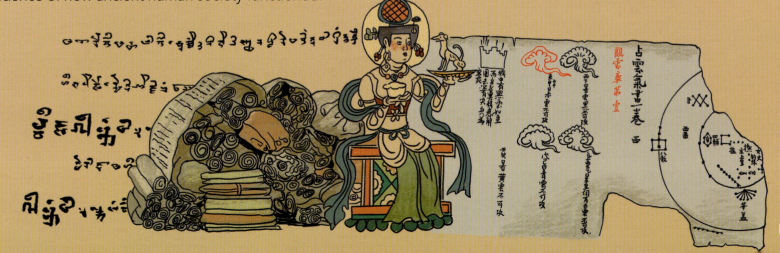

In 1907, Marc Aurel Stein from Britain arrived in Dunhuang and procured 29 cases of manuscripts and paintings from the Library Cave with just four silver ingots.

Sir Stein likes the murals depicting *Journey to the West*. He admires Master Xuanzang very much. He came here for true Buddhist scriptures.

All right, I'll bring you the scriptures. He can take what he wants.

I don't have time to sift through all of these. I'm taking all the Buddhist paintings with me and all the manuscripts in non-Han languages as well.

In 1908, Paul Pelliot from France arrived at the Mogao Caves and acquired the best parts of the Library Cave's treasures for only 500 taels of silver. Not until 1910 did the Qing government order the governor of Gansu to allocate funds to purchase and transport the manuscripts and paintings from the Library Cave to Beijing for safekeeping.

In 1921, hundreds of Russian refugees from the Russian Civil War resettled in Dunhuang, and the Mogao Caves were unexpectedly used as a prison. During the eight months prisoners lived in the caves, large areas of murals were blackened, smeared, and vandalized. It was the biggest catastrophe in the history of the Mogao Caves.

From 1907 to 1924, foreign treasure hunters such as Marc Aurel Stein, Paul Pelliot, Sergey Oldenburg, and Langdon Warner arrived in Dunhuang one after another. They lied and used silver to deal with Abbot Wang as they looted tons of treasures including tens of thousands of manuscripts, paintings, and even murals and sculptures.

The dispersal of Dunhuang manuscripts and artifacts around the world in a way facilitated the formation of a global academic discipline: Dunhuang Studies. In the 1930s and 1940s, more and more historians, archaeologists, and artists became devoted to the study of Dunhuang.

In 1944, National Dunhuang Art Institute was established with the famous painter Chang Shuhong as its first director. He led a group of enthusiastic young artists to protect and study the cultural heritage in Dunhuang.

In 1949, the founding of the People's Republic of China brought progress to work at National Dunhuang Art Research Institute. In 1950, the institute was renamed Dunhuang Cultural Relics Research Institute.

In 1984, the institute was expanded and renamed the Dunhuang Academy as the largest research entity for the protection and research of the Mogao Caves in the world.

In 1987, the Mogao Caves were inscribed on the UNESCO World Heritage List.

Today, the Dunhuang Academy is responsible for managing the Mogao Caves in Dunhuang, the Maijishan Grottoes in Tianshui, the Bingling Temple Grottoes in Yongjing, the Yulin Grottoes in Guazhou, the Western Thousand Buddha Caves in Dunhuang, and the Northern Caves in Qingyang. Of all cultural heritage management institutions, it manages the largest number of world cultural heritage sites in China.

In 1986, Dunhuang was listed as a National Historical and Cultural City.

In 2019, over 2 million visitors from around the world visited the Mogao Caves in Dunhuang.

Dunhuang witnessed the long history of the ancient Silk Road while looking forward to the future with new promises.

Neolithic Age
circa 2000 BC to 1000 BC

Period of contention among Wusun, Yuezhi, and Xiongnu
around the 2nd Century BC

Western Han Dynasty
121 BC–AD 8

Xinmang Dynasty
9–23

Eastern Han Dynasty
25–220

Wei of the Three Kingdoms period
220–265

Western Jin Dynasty
265–317

Eastern Jin Dynasty, 317–420
Former Liang Dynasty, 318–376
Former Qin Dynasty, 376–386
Later Liang Dynasty, 386–398
Northern Liang Dynasty, 398–400
Western Liang Dynasty, 400–421
Northern Liang Dynasty, 421–439

Northern Wei Dynasty
439–534

Western Wei Dynasty
535–556

Northern Zhou Dynasty
557–581

Sui Dynasty
581–618

Tang Dynasty, 618–907
Early Tang, 618–704
Grand Tang, 705–785
Mid Tang (Tibetan period), 786–847
Late Tang (Zhang-led Guiyi Army period), 848–907

Five Dynasties period, 907–960
Later Liang Dynasty, 907–923
Later Tang Dynasty, 923–936
Later Jin Dynasty, 936–947
Later Han Dynasty, 947–950
Later Zhou Dynasty, 951–960

Northern Song Dynasty
960–1035

Xixia Empire
1036–1227

Yuan Dynasty
1227–1368

Ming Dynasty
1368–1644

Qing Dynasty
1644–1911

Republic of China Period
1912–1949

People's Republic of China
1949 to present

Author's note:
The dynasties listed here indicate those that formally had Dunhuang under its jurisdiction, rather than the exact order and years of all the dynasties in ancient China before the Yuan Dynasty. For instance, the Western Han Dynasty started in 202 BC, while the chronology here shows 121 BC, which was the year when the Western Han authorities established prefectures in the region. For other instances of such discrepancy in the starting year of an ancient dynasty, please refer to the main text.

敦煌历史纪年表

新石器时代
约公元前 2000 年 — 约公元前 1000 年

乌孙、月氏、匈奴争夺期
约公元前 2 世纪

西汉
元狩二年（公元前 121 年）— 初始元年（8 年）

新莽
始建国元年（9 年）— 地皇四年（23 年）

东汉
建武元年（25 年）— 延康元年（220 年）

三国曹魏
黄初元年（220 年）— 咸熙二年（265 年）

西晋
泰始元年（265 年）— 建兴五年（317 年）

东晋 建武元年（317年）-元熙二年（420年）
前凉 建兴六年（318 年）— 咸安六年（376 年）
前秦 建元十二年（376 年）— 太安二年（386 年）
后凉 太安元年（386 年）— 龙飞三年（398 年）
北凉（段业）神玺二年（398 年）— 天玺二年（400 年）
西凉 庚子元年（400 年）— 永建二年（421 年）
北凉 玄始十年（421 年）— 永和七年（439 年）

北魏
太延五年（439 年）— 永熙三年（534 年）

西魏
大统元年（535 年）— 恭帝三年（556 年）

北周
宇文觉元年（557 年）— 大定元年（581 年）

隋
开皇元年（581 年）— 义宁二年（618 年）

唐 武德元年（618年）-天祐四年（907年）
初唐 武德元年（618 年）— 长安四年（704 年）
盛唐 神龙元年（705 年）— 贞元元年（785 年）
中唐（吐蕃时代）贞元二年（786 年）— 大中元年（847 年）
晚唐（张氏归义军）大中二年（848 年）— 天祐四年（907 年）

五代（西汉金山国至曹氏归义军前期）开平元年（907年）-显德七年（960年）
后梁 开平元年（907 年）— 龙德三年（923 年）
后唐 同光元年（923 年）— 清泰三年（936 年）
后晋 天福元年（936 年）— 开运四年（947 年）
后汉 天福十二年（947 年）— 乾祐三年（950 年）
后周 广顺元年（951 年）— 显德七年（960 年）

北宋（曹氏归义军后期）
建隆元年（960 年）— 景祐二年（1035 年）

西夏
大庆元年（1036 年）— 宝义元年（1227 年）

蒙古·元
成吉思汗二十二年（1227 年）— 至正二十八年（1368 年）

明
洪武元年（1368 年）— 崇祯十七年（1644 年）

清
顺治元年（1644 年）— 宣统三年（1911 年）

中华民国
1912 —1949 年

中华人民共和国
1949 年 10 月 1 日至今

作者注
　　本表中，元代及元代之前朝代的起止时间为其实际统治敦煌的时间；而明代至中华民国时期敦煌地方形势较为复杂，故仅标出全国统一的朝代分期，具体情况见正文。

附录：中文全文

今天，我们一起出发去敦煌喽！

那里有世界文化遗产莫高窟，可以看到中国古代最精美的壁画。

那里有鸣沙山和月牙泉，可以骑着骆驼在大漠中行走。

品尝葡萄、李广杏、甜瓜……每一种水果都是一段甜蜜的回忆。

敦煌，是古丝绸之路的咽喉重镇，曾是东西方文明交汇的枢纽。

现在的敦煌是我国西北部的一座小城市。可是在古代，这里可是赫赫有名的大都会。

那时敦煌的地域范围很大，包括党河流域和疏勒河流域的广大地区，是中原通往西域的必经之地。

"大叔，出了这个门您就走上阳关大道了，这批丝绸运到大秦（指罗马帝国）一定能大赚一笔！"

"小朋友，过了这个门就进敦煌了，这地儿可好玩儿了，你的通行证呢？"

早在新石器时代，敦煌就有人类生活。这里出土了约公元前1600年的生产生活工具、农作物，发现了约公元前1000年的房屋遗址。

那时的人们，使用石刀、石锛（bēn）进行农业生产，种植麦、粟、黍等农作物。

他们还制作陶器作为生活用具，还有乐器陶埙（xūn）。

P7 早期人们以石镞（zú）为箭头进行狩猎，大量使用方便携带的细石器，捕获野生的牛、鹿、黄羊、羚羊等动物。

P8 据文字记载，敦煌最早是游牧民族繁衍生息的地方，乌孙人、月氏（zhī）人都曾在这里生活。

秦汉之际，月氏人与乌孙人交战，杀掉了乌孙首领，迫使乌孙人向西迁徙到天山以北。

P9 公元前2世纪初期，匈奴人强大起来，他们击败月氏人，占据了河西走廊和西域。

大部分月氏人被迫西迁到伊犁河流域，被称作"大月氏"；继续留在敦煌附近生活的，被称作"小月氏"。

P10 西汉初年，匈奴人不断侵扰汉朝北部边界，占据着河西走廊，阻碍着中原与西域的交通。

公元前121年，西汉大将霍去病两次带兵重创匈奴，收复了河西地区，置武威、酒泉二郡。

P11 建元二年（前139年），张骞（qiān）受汉武帝派遣出使西域。他带着一百多人的使团从长安出发，西行进入河西走廊后被匈奴人扣押。
直到元光六年（前129年）张骞才逃脱，继续西行至大宛（yuān），经康居，抵达大月氏，再至大夏，停留了一年多返回。
在归途中，张骞再次被匈奴人抓获。元朔三年（前126年）匈奴内乱，张骞才带着他的匈奴妻子和助手甘父乘机逃回汉朝。

这次出使，第一次使中原和西域有了直接交往，因此也被称为"张骞凿空"。

P12 公元前111年，西汉分武威、酒泉两郡，增设张掖（yè）、敦煌，并将长城从酒泉修筑到敦煌以西，在敦煌郡城西面设玉门关和阳关，完成了"列四郡，据两关"之势。从此，敦煌正式成为中原通往西域的门户和边防军事重镇。

"再也不怕匈奴人来打劫了！"

P13 这里是河仓城，是西汉在敦煌储备军需的大仓库。官兵将士从这里领取粮食、衣物和草料，以保证给养，鼓舞士气。

这里是马圈湾烽燧（suì），是古代用来传递警报的重要建筑。如果观察到有外敌入侵，士兵就点燃烽火，告诉大家敌人的数量、远近和军情紧急程度。

这里是悬泉置，是汉代的邮驿机构。和现在的邮局不同，这里不仅负责传递官府的文件，还为过往的官员和使者提供食宿、车辆、马匹和草料。

P14 西汉的敦煌郡包括六个县——敦煌、龙勒、效谷、广至、渊泉、冥安，郡治敦煌。这些县名都很有趣，有几个还有特别的意义。

敦煌县。"敦，大也；煌，盛也"，"敦煌"形容这里盛大辉煌。
龙勒县。史载，河南新野人暴利长因罪被罚在敦煌放马，他用勒马索抓住天马，献给了汉武帝。天马被认为是龙驹，所以抓住天马的地方就被称为"龙勒"。

P15 效谷县。以前这里被称为"渔泽障"，汉武帝时都尉崔不意教百姓开垦田地，以勤效得谷，故名"效谷"。
渊泉县因当地泉水特别多而得名，看来敦煌在古代不像现在这么干旱哟！

汉武帝多次将内地的居民迁移到这里，并组织移民和士兵开垦土地、种植粮食。敦煌逐渐成为中原王朝经营西域、交通贸易的重要基地。

P16 西汉末年，王莽篡位，中原大乱，包括敦煌在内的河西地区也危机四伏。自愿到河西为官的窦融，因懂得团结各族人民、抚慰百姓被推举为河西五郡（汉昭帝时在河西四郡基础上增设金城郡，合称"河西五郡"）大将军。

P17 在他的带领下，河西不仅抵御了羌、匈奴的侵扰，还发展了农业和畜牧业，成为避乱者乐于投奔的安居之地。

"世道这么乱，我要找一个地方让母亲安度晚年，河西最合适！"
"关中粮价太贵了，一石（dàn）米都要两千钱了！河西一石米才两百钱，咱们都到河西安家吧！"

P18 东汉时期（25—220年），北匈奴崛起，敦煌成为汉王朝统领西域的军政中心。东汉中后期，主管西域事务的护西域副校尉常驻敦煌。

永和二年（137年），北匈奴袭扰西域，敦煌太守裴岑率兵三千人前往西域迎击。
裴岑在蒲类海大获全胜并立《裴岑纪功碑》纪念这次胜利。

P19 当时敦煌有位多次打败匈奴、屡立战功的名将，名叫张奂。他也是当时著名的学者。
张奂的长子就是被誉为"草圣"的书法家张芝。张芝从小在水池边练习书法，整池水都被墨染黑。

这时敦煌还出现了一个叫"小浮屠里"的地方，"浮屠"是佛陀或佛塔的音译，说明佛教这时已传入敦煌。

P20 三国魏文帝曹丕时，河西继续实行西汉以来的屯戍（shù）政策，促进了敦煌地区社会经济的发展。太和元年（227年），仓慈继任敦煌太守。
他上任后，打压抑制当地的豪强大族，维护了敦煌的安定繁荣。

"请把土地分给没有田地的百姓耕种！"
"积压这么多年的案子要公正快速地审完！"
"不能让豪强敲诈胡商，必要时请派兵保护商队！"

P21 嘉平元年（249年），皇甫隆出任敦煌太守，大力推广中原的先进生产工具和耕作技术，大大提高了敦煌的农作物产量，还改变了敦煌妇女做一条裙子要用一匹布的旧俗。

这里以前的农耕技术太落后了，现在有了楼（lóu）犁和衍溉法，省了一半的力不说，还多收了五成的粮食！
楼犁是古代耕种用的农具，可以一边开沟一边播种，实在是太方便了！
原来做一条羊肠大裙就要用掉一匹布！现在这款裙子多好，又省布又轻便！

P22 西晋初年，东吴降将吾彦调任敦煌太守。他在敦煌镇守数年，亲自带领百姓耕种，鼓励大家积极生产，延续了敦煌经济的繁荣。

敦煌名僧竺（zhú）法护，八岁出家，遍游西域，通晓多种语言。晋武帝时，他携带大量佛经东归，从敦煌前往长安，沿路翻译佛经并传播佛法。

太康五年（284年），竺法护回到敦煌，在弟子和信众的协助下，完成《修行道地经》和《阿惟越致遮经》的翻译。竺法护一生共翻译佛经165部，被当时的人们称为"敦煌菩萨"。

P23 这时敦煌文化发达，出现了一批著名学者。

敦煌郡的索靖、汜（fán）衷、张魁（hán）、索绗（zhěn）、索永一同入太学学习，号称"敦煌五龙"。

索靖为敦煌龙勒人，是西晋著名的将领和学者。索靖擅长草书，还是一位书法理论家，著有《草书状》。
游览鸣沙山后，他还在莫高窟的崖面上题写过"仙岩寺"三个大字（现已不存）。

P24 西晋末年，中原大乱，前来河西避难的人日月相继。他们的到来不仅补充了敦煌的劳动力，还带来了中原的文化和技术。

永宁元年（301年），张轨出任凉州刺史。他到任后，重视农业和教育，安置流民，提拔贤才，使河西稳步发展。

此时，任敦煌太守的阴澹（dàn）在敦煌城西南修七里长渠用于灌溉。当地百姓受益不尽，将此渠称为"阴安渠"。

P25 东晋永和元年（345年），凉州牧张骏将敦煌、晋昌、高昌三郡和西域都护、戊己校尉、玉门大护军三营合并成沙州，治所敦煌，任命西胡校尉杨宣为刺史。
杨宣任内，曾组织民众兴修水利，建五石斗门，堰水溉田，在原来平渠的基础上，重建成十五里的"阳（杨）开渠"。

这时候敦煌人习惯在墓室的墙砖上绘画，不仅绘出各种奇禽异兽，还绘出农耕、采摘、畜牧、屠宰、烹饪、宴饮、出行等各种日常生活的画面。

P26 前秦建元二年（366年），一个名叫乐僔（zǔn）的和尚来到鸣沙山的断崖前，他面前忽然出现了万道金光，其中仿佛有千佛闪耀，于是他在这里开凿了莫高窟的第一个洞窟。

建元十二年（376年），前秦灭前凉，将包括敦煌在内的河西地区归入治下。前秦皇帝符（fú）坚把江汉、中原百姓一万七千余户迁到敦煌，促进了敦煌地区的开发。

P27 前秦大将吕光从龟兹带回了著名的翻译家、高僧鸠摩罗什。途中，鸠摩罗什的坐骑白马在敦煌病死。相传现在敦煌市城西的白马塔就是为了纪念它。

"我昨晚梦见小白跑来告诉我，它是佛祖派来送我去东土传法的。现在任务完成了，它也要离开了！"

苻坚死后，吕光割据凉州，建立了后凉政权。麟嘉七年（395年），后凉内乱，西奔敦煌地区的人有数千户，又一次为这里输入了大量的人力。

后凉的敦煌太守孟敏主持修建了敦煌城南的水渠，人称"孟授渠"。孟敏去世后，百姓在城西五里立"孟庙"纪念他。

P28　东晋隆安四年（400年），敦煌太守李暠（hào）被推举为大将军、凉公，建立西凉政权。西凉定都敦煌，敦煌在历史上第一次成为都城。

西凉建立了县、乡、里三级行政管理机构，实行严密的编户制度，并鼓励生产。

敦煌地区出现了五谷丰登、百姓乐业的景象。

P29　李暠在敦煌城内为其父立先王庙，设立了官方学府泮（pàn）官，学生多达五百人。于阗（tián）、鄯（shàn）善等西域王国也来此朝贡，敦煌已然有都城之派。

但卢水胡人沮渠蒙逊建立的北凉政权对西凉构成很大威胁，于是李暠于西凉建初元年（405年）迁都酒泉与之对抗。同时带走了两万三千户，敦煌实力大为削弱。

迁都酒泉后，西凉加强了敦煌的防守，修复了多段旧塞城墙以防御外敌。

"敦煌是个全国有名的地方，百姓忠厚，文人辈出。儿子你一定要施行利于百姓的政策！"

P30　西凉嘉兴四年（420年），北凉大败西凉。北凉国君沮渠蒙逊派喜好杀戮的索元绪任敦煌太守，不得人心。敦煌郡的宋承、张弘等人联合原西凉敦煌太守李恂（xún）赶走了索元绪。

李恂被推举为冠军将军、凉州刺史，面对沮渠蒙逊派来的大军，李恂闭门不战，坚守敦煌。421年，沮渠蒙逊亲自率兵攻城。李恂兵败自杀，沮渠蒙逊纵兵屠城。一时敦煌城毁人亡，满目疮痍。

P31 沮渠蒙逊虽然是匈奴后裔，但重视汉文化，身边笼络不少敦煌文人。阚骃（kàn yīn）、宋繇（yáo）、刘昞（bǐng）都继续受到重用，刘昞后来还被尊为国师。

"咱们都是一家人！"

这一时期营建了莫高窟现存年代最早的三个洞窟，即现在编号为268、272和275的"北凉三窟"，是集禅修、礼拜和讲经说法为一体的禅室、佛殿和佛堂的组合。

P32 北魏太延五年（439年），北魏灭北凉，原北凉的酒泉太守沮渠无讳（huì）逃到敦煌继续抵抗。三年后，沮渠无讳撤离敦煌，带走了万余户聚集敦煌的河西精英。在北凉灭西凉和北魏灭北凉的两次兵祸之中，敦煌遭到了前所未有的破坏。

同年，李暠之孙李宝占据敦煌，归降北魏，被封为沙州牧、敦煌公。他修复城池，安置流民，敦煌重新获得了安定。

太平真君五年（444年），为经营西域和抗击北方的柔然，北魏直接控制敦煌，建敦煌镇。两次从敦煌发兵西域，丝绸之路再次打通，西域商人纷纷前来贸易。

P33 北魏献文帝时，柔然控制了西域。敦煌成为抗击柔然的前沿阵地。敦煌军民在镇将尉多侯、乐洛生的率领下，几败柔然，保住了敦煌。

北魏太和九年（485年），穆亮任敦煌镇都大将，他为政宽简，赈恤穷乏，敦煌经济得到恢复。但常年征战，人口流失，人力物力的损失很难迅速恢复。

P34 正光五年（524年），北魏改敦煌镇为瓜州。因为日照时间长、昼夜温差大，所以敦煌水果糖分含量高，味道特别甜。"瓜州"就是因敦煌盛产好吃的甜瓜而来。北魏派皇族元荣出任瓜州刺史，治理敦煌近二十年。他团结豪右，保境安民，出资写经十余部，还在莫高窟开凿大型洞窟。

这一时期，敦煌壁画以故事画见长，最为著名的九色鹿连环画《鹿王本生图》就出自北魏莫高窟第257窟。

P35 元荣在西魏时继续任职，主持开凿了著名的"东阳王窟"，即莫高窟第285窟。这时的壁画出现了褒衣博带、秀骨清像的人物形象，应是元荣从中原带来的新风格。

"以前，敦煌壁画受西域的影响，人物都是粗壮健硕的模样。"
"你看起来好瘦啊，你的衣服好大啊！又瘦又飘逸，这是中原的新潮流吧！"

P36 北周初年的敦煌太守令狐休，为人清廉节俭，推行奖励农耕的政策，把敦煌治理得井井有条。中原和西域的交通畅通无阻，敦煌的各项事业都呈上升发展的趋势。

建平郡公于义任瓜州刺史时继续在莫高窟开窟造像，莫高窟第428窟被认为是他带领沙州和凉州的僧侣、百姓共一千多人集资开凿的。

P37 这幅画是西域商旅通行丝路的场景，你看右边牵骆驼商人的大鼻子，他是一位典型"胡商"。"胡商"在那时主要指中亚的粟特商人。

"我面前的四方形柱叫作'中心塔柱'，有这种方柱的洞窟叫'中心柱窟'。"

P38 隋代，全国重新统一在强大的中央王朝之下。大业三年（607年），改瓜州为敦煌郡。但这时西域商人多到张掖进行贸易活动。

隋代大臣裴矩根据自己掌管张掖贸易市场时搜集到的信息，写了《西域图记》一书，内容包括四十四国山川、姓氏、风土、服饰、物产等信息，并绘有地图。

"你是康国来的，给我讲讲你们康国的故事！这位兄弟是波斯来的，快给我介绍介绍你们波斯的特产！"
"我们波斯盛产精美织锦……"
"我们是最擅长贩运货物的商人……"

P39　隋代通西域的道路共有三条，北道、中道和南道，这三条道路在敦煌汇合。这就是敦煌被称为"丝绸之路的咽喉之地"的原因。

大业年间，西域高昌、康国、安国等三十多国使者先后来朝，贡献大量西域特产。隋朝使节也从西域带回各种方物。随着中原和西域的使团、商队往来增多，敦煌作为西域和中原经济文化交流中转站的地位日渐恢复。

高昌贡上赤盐和葡萄酒，康国贡上阿萨那香，龟兹贡上安息香和良马，于阗贡上美玉，吐火罗贡上神马……

"我从安国带回了五色盐，从罽（jì）宾带回了玛瑙，这是史国的舞女……"

P40　隋代皇帝信奉佛教，促进了敦煌佛教的发展。隋文帝曾令天下各州起塔供奉舍利，莫高窟的崇教寺也在其列。

隋代不仅在莫高窟开凿了大批的洞窟，藏经洞还出土了皇室成员的写经，可见隋王朝对敦煌的重视。
这里有隋秦王妃崔氏写的《思益经》，隋独孤皇后写的《大楼炭经》《太子慕魄经》，还有隋炀帝当太子时写的《大般涅槃经》呢！

P41　随着纺织和印染技术的发展，隋代已能生产出纹样精美的丝绸。此时许多西域锦缎纹样沿丝绸之路向中原传播，隋代服饰的纹样更丰富了！

"这个洞窟的佛像真高大！"

联珠纹是当时波斯织锦的代表纹样。这种纹样是由一串彼此相连的圆形或球形组成，圈中还绘以凤鸟、猛虎、狮子、大象、翼马、花卉等，整个图案显得生动活泼。这些时髦的纹样很快就进入了中国市场。

P42 隋末唐初，敦煌地区动荡不安，内有割据势力为乱，外有突厥等势力侵扰。

"我不给唐朝打工当什么瓜州刺史了，我要当敦煌王！"
"我爱大唐，决斗吧！"
"我们也不想给唐朝打工，窦伏明你来当我们的头儿！"
"看眼前的形势，大家还是跟我一起投唐吧！"
"占了西沙州，继续打瓜州！"
"我爱大唐！想占瓜州没门！"

P43 唐初西域处于西突厥的管控之下，周边吐谷（yù）浑、吐蕃（bō）都对瓜州虎视眈眈。故武德末、贞观初，唐朝关闭西北关津，不许百姓于此出境。贞观年间玄奘（zàng）西行求法之时，实际上是从瓜州偷渡出去的。

由于武则天崇信佛教，敦煌的佛事更盛。藏经洞保存了武则天组织抄写的官廷写经《法华经》和《金刚经》。为了迎合武则天是弥勒降世的社会舆论，在禅师灵隐和居士阴祖的组织下，敦煌还营建了高达35.5米的弥勒大佛（北大像），这也是莫高窟最大的佛像。

P44 贞观之后，中原文化频繁西传，莫高窟艺术进入了一个新时期。莫高窟第220窟的壁画中，不仅再现了中原长安佛寺的景象，还有唐朝皇帝、各国首领和使者的肖像，大唐王朝贞观盛世的景象就这样被定格在敦煌的一个洞窟当中。

唐代是中原和西域乐舞艺术大交流、大融合的昌盛时期，这时官廷和民间广泛流传从西域传来的舞蹈。壁画下方的这四名舞伎，两两相对起舞，这种节奏欢快的舞蹈就是西域传来的。

P45 这位坐在帐中的老者是维摩诘（jié），他精通大乘佛法且家财万贯。他正在跟佛教中智慧第一的文殊菩萨辩论。著名的唐代大诗人王维字摩诘，就是取维摩诘之意。

来听辩论的人真多啊！文殊这边有唐朝的皇帝，你看他头戴冕旒（liú），肩上有日月，这是只有皇帝才能穿的服装！

维摩诘这边是各国首领和使者。那位戴高帽、穿锦袍的是波斯王子，这位冠上插了两根鹖（hé）羽的使者来自朝鲜半岛。当时唐朝与东西各国的往来十分密切！

P46 盛唐时期，虽然西北地区战事频繁，但在国力蒸蒸日上的环境下，敦煌仍然得到了充分的发展。唐王朝通过县、乡、里各级政权组织和完备的户籍制度对敦煌地区实行有效的管理和严密的控制。

"效谷乡索詈（lì）才，年十五，家有五十六岁寡母，应授田、已授田、永业田、口分田、居住院宅和未授田数，均已登记完毕！"

唐代从高宗、武后至玄宗时期，一直都在河陇地区大兴屯田，敦煌农业得到了长足的发展。水渠灌溉系统得到完善，仅敦煌县就有6条主干渠、116条支渠，组成了强大的水利网。
同时，还配之以严密的管水配水制度，对水资源进行管理。

P47 "大家都说现在天下最富庶的地方就是陇右！"
"咱们敦煌也在这个范围内！"

当时敦煌市场上，有来自中原的丝绸、瓷器，也有来自西域的玉石、珍宝；有北方的驼马、毛织品，也有本地盛产的五谷，商品经济繁荣。东来西往的使者、商贾、僧侣、百姓，源源不断地通过敦煌往来于中原与西域，中国与印度、西亚之间。

"胡商中数我们粟特商人最多，城东的从化乡是专门给我们的定居点！"

"做生意就是互通有无，敦煌市场绝对国际范儿！"

P48 在这样的背景下，莫高窟也迎来了全盛时期。此时窟龛（kān）达一千余所，景象蔚为壮观。这一时期的敦煌艺术与中原唐风一脉相承，彩塑注重人体比例与人物性格的表达，壁画里描绘的佛国世界则是现实社会的真实写照。

这是敦煌最精美最完整的一组塑像，佛祖坐在正中间，离他最近的是一老一少两位弟子，其次是亭亭玉立的两位菩萨，最外侧是怒目圆睁的两位天王。仅仅通过他们的表情，我们就仿佛看到了他们的内心世界。

P49 这些胡商在贩运货物的路上遇到了强盗，他们丢在地上的货物里，有一捆丝绸！那时人人都爱中国的丝绸，它们绝对是丝路上的"硬通货"！

下雨了，农民伯伯还在地里辛勤劳作！

你看那坐在田边吃饭的一家三口多么温馨！

P50 天宝十四年（755年）安史之乱爆发后，唐王朝将西北精锐部队调到中原，吐蕃乘机占领陇右、河西的大片土地。

"大人，城里没有粮食了！军械也耗尽了！"

"告诉你们主帅，如果不把敦煌人迁徙到其他地方，我们愿意开城投降！"

"同意！"

贞元二年（786年），沙州以"勿徙（xǐ）他境"为条件，与吐蕃结城下之盟，开始吐蕃统治敦煌的中唐时期。

吐蕃占领敦煌初期，推行蕃化政策，要求敦煌汉人穿吐蕃装、说吐蕃话。这些政策引起敦煌人极大的反感，并引发了玉关驿户起义。

P51 敦煌的动荡引起了吐蕃上层的反思，于是转而利用当地的世家大族进行统治以缓和民族矛盾，并大力扶持佛教，借用宗教的力量来稳定局势。

这时敦煌佛教空前繁荣，寺院从十三所增加到十七所。出家人中有不少是不愿与吐蕃合作的唐朝官员和大族子弟，僧侣的文化水平得到了很大提高。很多僧人还积极参与政务，成为维护敦煌安定的重要力量。

"我堂堂大唐法曹参军，不能当吐蕃的官，出家去！"
"在吐蕃出家人也能参与政事，给赞普当顾问！"

敦煌高僧摩诃（hē）衍甚至到吐蕃王廷传播禅宗教义，引起了关于"顿渐之争"的佛教大辩论——吐蕃僧诤会。

莲花戒："渐悟！"
摩诃衍："顿悟！"

P52 大中二年（848年），敦煌人张议潮趁吐蕃内乱，率众起义。经过浴血奋战，张议潮等人一举收复瓜、沙二州。之后，他们又收复了肃、甘、伊等州。

大中五年（851年），受张议潮的委派，他的兄长张议潭携带河西陇右十一州图籍抵达长安向唐宣宗告捷。

"自古关西出将，这话一点儿不假！"

P53 这一年，唐王朝任命张议潮为归义军节度使，敦煌正式进入归义军时期。至咸通七年（866年）十月，归义军辖区终于"西尽伊吾，东接灵武，得地四千余里，户口百万之家，六郡山河，宛然而旧"！
咸通八年（867年），为了避免朝廷的猜忌，张议潮入居长安终老。在继任者问题上，归义军政权内部矛盾重重。经历了张、索、李等各大家族的争夺之后，到张承奉坐上了节度使之位时，归义军的有效辖区实际上只

14

剩下了瓜、沙二州。

P54 后梁开平三年（909年），张承奉得知唐朝灭亡后，自称白衣天子，建立西汉金山国。"西汉"意为西部汉人之国，"金山"即敦煌境内的"金鞍山"。

"大唐没了，我们归义军怎么办？"
"坊间流行《白雀歌》，白雀是祥瑞之兆，您当称帝立国。"

金山国虽锐意进取，想收复失地，但在战争中屡遭失败。911年，回鹘（hú）大举进攻，金山国由于连年战争国力衰微，不得不与回鹘立城下之盟：回鹘可汗是父，金山国天子是子。

乾化四年（914年），出身敦煌另一大族的曹议金取代张承奉。曹议金认为必须要倚仗中原王朝的威势才能震慑局势，于是奉中原为正朔，自称"归义军节度兵马留后"。

P55 曹议金一方面注重与周边政权联姻，将两个女儿分别嫁给了甘州回鹘可汗和于阗王；另一方面积极吸收名门望族和少数民族头领参与归义军政权，得到境内军民的广泛支持。
"甘州、于阗一东一西，都要搞好关系！"
"岳父！"
"岳父！"

由于曹议金内外关系处理得当，此时归义军实力有所恢复。敦煌仍是丝绸之路的重要中转站，市场上充满来自东西方的商品。

"我们铺里有：橘皮胡桃瓤，栀子高良姜，陆路诃黎勒，大腹及槟榔;亦有莳（shí）萝荜拨，芜荑（yí）大黄，油麻椒蒜，河藕佛香；甜干枣，醋石榴；绢帽子，罗幞（fú）头；白矾（fán）皂矾，紫草苏芳；䬾糖吃时牙齿美，饧（xíng）糖咬时舌头甜；市上买取新祆子，街头易得紫罗衫；阔口裤，崭新鞋，大胯腰带十三事……"

P56 曹议金之后，敦煌归义军政权一直由曹氏家族把持。其中，曹议金第三子曹元忠在位时间最长，他积极发展与周边民族的关系，同时与中原王朝保持联系，为敦煌带来一段安定繁荣的时光。

曹氏笃信佛教，这时官方设立画院，有能力营建大型洞窟。曹元忠主持营建了莫高窟的文殊堂，修缮了北大像。

"夫人，北大像下层的木结构年久失修，需要修修了！"
"夫君，我要亲自做饭，慰劳工匠！"

P57 著名的印度高僧法贤等人路过敦煌时，被节度使曹延禄扣留数月，请求他们在本地传法。后来高僧们只好把锡杖、钵盂（bō yú）等随身物品丢弃，只带着一些佛经离开敦煌。

曹元忠以后，归义军政权逐步衰落，内忧外患。11世纪初的某一天，敦煌人将大量的佛经、佛画及其他文物封存进了一个洞窟，并砌堵窟门、绘制壁画进行掩饰，这个窟就是后来的"藏经洞"。

P58 归义军晚期沙州回鹘势力崛起，约于北宋天圣八年（1030年）取代曹氏政权。这一时期的敦煌石窟中，出现了身穿龙袍的回鹘可汗像。

P59 北宋景祐三年（1036年），党项攻占敦煌，仍称沙州。两年后，党项建立西夏政权，一直与宋、辽争战，无暇西顾，对敦煌的控制很薄弱。所以不少人认为这时敦煌的实际统治者是沙州回鹘。

"宣使臣上殿！"

北宋天圣元年（1023年）至皇祐二年（1050年），沙州地方政权曾先后七次向北宋朝贡。

P60 北宋宝元元年（1038年），党项李元昊称帝建国，史称西夏。约西夏乾道元年（1068年），西夏加强了对瓜、沙二州的直接控制。这时榆林窟成为西夏重点营建的石窟。

"这里是佛教圣宫，这个洞窟是我们赵家的功德窟。这是国师西壁智海，把他的真容画在墙上一定能够保佑我们全家平安！"

西夏大安八年（1082年），为了和北宋进行战争，西夏曾从瓜、沙地区大规模征调百姓。西夏贞观十年（1110年），瓜、沙、肃三州发生饥荒，百姓流亡他乡。这些都使敦煌的社会经济一度遭到削弱。

P61 由于西夏的阻隔，来自西方的使者和商人纷纷避开敦煌，改从青海或蒙古草原进入中原。敦煌逐渐失去了丝路贸易中转站的地位。

"西夏收的税太高，我们不走敦煌了，改从青海道走！"
"西夏占着敦煌，我们也改走北方的蒙古草原了！"

西夏统治者重视佛教，从周边地区吸收多元的佛教文化，这时的石窟大胆创新，呈现出多种艺术风格。西夏晚期还引入了藏传密教，营建了莫高窟第一个藏密洞窟。

P62 1227年，蒙古灭西夏，占领敦煌，将其划入成吉思汗之孙拔都的封地。至元十四年（1277年），忽必烈将敦煌收归中央政府直接管辖，重新设置沙州。

敦煌再次成为河西交通线上的重要补给站。元朝建立后不久，意大利人马可·波罗途经敦煌。

"居民主要从事农耕，这里盛产小麦。沙州城中有许多寺院，供奉着各种各样的佛像。埋葬死者要请占卜者来挑选日子，下葬时准备大量的纸人纸马，还一直伴随着嘈杂的乐声。"

P63 至元十七年（1280年），沙州升格为路，设总管府。至元二十九年（1292年），元朝从沙州、瓜州往甘州强制移民，瓜、沙地区一度荒芜。

元成宗时重新派兵驻守瓜、沙地区。元朝常以宗室诸王驻镇管理敦煌，并注重扶持和利用佛教维护统治。

镇守沙州的西宁王速来蛮家族在莫高窟刻立了《六字真言碣（jié）》，其继任者牙罕沙重修了莫高窟皇庆寺。

P64 1368年，明朝建立。洪武五年（1372年），明将冯胜在肃州西七十里处建嘉峪关，作为明朝西部边关。嘉峪关通哈密之路成为中原与西域交通的主要通道，敦煌被弃置关外。

此后，明朝通过册封蒙古后裔间接管理敦煌等地，先后设立"关西七卫"，形成隔绝西部威胁的缓冲屏障。

"我们请求归附大明！"
"在敦煌设沙州卫，任命困即来和买住为指挥使！"

P65 永乐二年（1404年）设沙州卫，成化十五年（1479年）又在沙州故城置罕东卫。但由于内忧外患不断，明朝时期敦煌在文化上没有多少建树，莫高窟也没有新修洞窟。

"都别打了，安分守沙州！"
"继任的沙州卫指挥使喃哥兄弟打起来了！"

正德十一年（1516年），敦煌被吐鲁番贵族占领。由于当地百姓多次被迁入内地，至此敦煌人口空虚，本地文化传承几近断绝。因无人管理，莫高窟不少下层窟龛被风沙掩埋，佛像也屡遭破坏，满目凄凉。

P66 "老乡，你住哪儿？"
"我住岷（mín）州坊，我们从岷州搬过来的。"

1644年明亡，清兵入关，清朝定都北京。清朝在康熙时开始经营西域，嘉峪关以西的广大地区逐渐恢复。雍正元年（1723年）在敦煌设沙州所，后升格为卫。

在川陕总督岳钟琪的建议下，清朝从甘肃迁移2400余户百姓到敦煌屯田，由政府借给耕牛、农具、种子及七个月的口粮，给每户划分空地、发三两银子盖房，并按原籍分区进行管理，以原来的州县名命名安置地。

"疆宇新开增气象，边民辐辏（còu）往来通。"

雍正五年（1727年），光禄少卿汪隆来敦煌监理新城、衙署和兵房的修建。

P67 乾隆二十五年（1760年），升沙州卫为敦煌县。实行移民屯田之后，敦煌的经济开始复苏。农耕又成为当地的主要生产方式，水利建设也日益完善，人口增长迅速，莫高窟也重新见到香火。

嘉庆和道光年间，敦煌的佛教徒对莫高窟进行了大规模整修，针对当时百姓的信仰将一些洞窟进行改造，但艺术水平相对较低。

"快来快来，快拜拜送子娘娘，来年得个大胖娃娃！"

同治年间，西北地区爆发起义，敦煌一度成为战场，人口因此减少，经济上再次遭受打击。

P68 19世纪末，道士王圆箓来到莫高窟。这时，莫高窟看起来有些荒凉，崖面上的栈道多已不存在，底层洞窟很多都堆起积沙。

"我用烟袋锅敲了敲，有回音，里面一定有个洞！"
"咱们快扒开看看！哎呀，这么多值钱的古物！"

王道士于是自作主张当起了莫高窟的住持，用得到的香火钱按自己的想法整修洞窟。光绪二十六年（1900年），他在清理积沙的过程中意外发现了"藏经洞"。

P69

起初，王道士拿出部分写卷、佛画等分赠当地官员和乡绅，并未引起重视。1904年，甘肃布政司命敦煌县令汪宗翰将藏经洞文物就地封存，并责令王道士妥善保管，不许外流。

敦煌藏经洞为20世纪初最重要的考古大发现之一。藏经洞内保存了近七万件古代各类文献。除大量佛经以外，还有极具价值的官私文书和少数民族文字资料。

藏经洞艺术品主要有绢画、麻布画、纸画等，还有丝织品如彩幡（fān）、刺绣等，以及木雕艺术品。这些文献和文物反映了古代社会的方方面面，有着无法估量的价值。

P70

1907年，英国的斯坦因来到敦煌，用四个马蹄银从王道士手中换取了29箱藏经洞文物。

"斯大人说墙上的《西游记》壁画很好，他很崇拜里面的唐僧，他来这儿就是为了求取真经的。"
"好，我把经书拿出来让他挑！"

1908年，法国的伯希和来到了莫高窟，他用500两白银换取了藏经洞宝藏的精华。直到1910年，清学部才电令甘肃，拨款购买并运送藏经洞文献到北京收藏。

"我时间有限，所有佛画我要带走，非汉文的经卷也全部带走！"

P71

1921年，在苏俄国内战争中失败的数百名白俄匪军被安置到敦煌，莫高窟竟被当作天然监狱。他们在洞窟内生活了8个多月，烧炕、做饭，大量壁画被熏黑、涂抹、刻画，成为莫高窟历史上最大的劫难。

1907—1924年，先后闻讯而来的外国盗宝者斯坦因、伯希和、奥登堡和华尔纳等人，以谎言加白银，先后向王道士骗取数万件文献、大量绘画品，甚至还有莫高窟内的壁画、彩塑等其他文物。

P72 敦煌文献文物流散于世界各地，间接促进了一门世界性的显学——敦煌学的形成。自20世纪三四十年代开始，越来越多历史学、考古学和美术工作者投身到敦煌学的研究事业，莫高窟的知名度也越来越高。

1944年，国立敦煌艺术研究所成立，由法国归来的画家常书鸿任首任所长。他率领一批有志青年担负起保护洞窟、临摹壁画、研究敦煌文化的重任。

P73 1949年，新中国成立，敦煌艺术研究所的文物保护和研究工作全面开展起来。1950年，敦煌艺术研究所更名为敦煌文物研究所。

1984年，敦煌文物研究所扩建为敦煌研究院，成为全世界最大的敦煌石窟保护研究的科研实体。

1987年，莫高窟被联合国教科文组织列入"世界文化遗产名录"。

现在，敦煌研究院负责管理敦煌莫高窟、天水麦积山石窟、永靖炳灵寺石窟、瓜州榆林窟、敦煌西千佛洞和庆阳北石窟寺，是我国拥有世界文化遗产数量最多、跨区域范围最广的文博管理机构。

1986年，敦煌被命名为"国家历史文化名城"。

2019年，敦煌莫高窟迎接全世界游客超过200万人次！

今天，敦煌这颗古老丝绸之路上的明珠，正以全新的面貌迎接世界。

图书在版编目（CIP）数据

敦煌：从新石器时代到今天：汉英对照／赵晓星
著；李朝渊译．-- 北京：朝华出版社，2024.6
ISBN 978-7-5054-5343-2

Ⅰ．①敦… Ⅱ．①赵… ②李… Ⅲ．①敦煌学－少儿
读物－汉、英 Ⅳ．① K870.6-49

中国国家版本馆 CIP 数据核字（2024）第 089192 号

敦煌：从新石器时代到今天

撰　　文　赵晓星
绘　　图　撒旦君
翻　　译　李朝渊
审　　定　[美] 斯科特·亨茨曼（Scott Huntsman）

出 版 人　汪　涛
责任编辑　张　璇
执行编辑　范佳铖
责任印制　陆竞赢　崔　航
排版制作　刘洁琼

出版发行　朝华出版社
社　　址　北京市西城区百万庄大街 24 号　　　邮政编码　100037
订购电话　(010) 68996522
传　　真　(010) 88415258（发行部）
联系版权　zhbq@cicg.org.cn
网　　址　http://zhcb.cicg.org.cn
印　　刷　天津联城印刷有限公司
经　　销　全国新华书店
开　　本　889mm×1194mm　1/16　　　　　字　　数　85 千字
印　　张　6.5
版　　次　2024 年 6 月第 1 版　2024 年 6 月第 1 次印刷
装　　别　平
书　　号　ISBN 978-7-5054-5343-2
定　　价　78.00 元

First Edition in June 2024, First Printing in June 2024

Dunhuang: From the Neolithic Age to Today

Written by Zhao Xiaoxing

Illustrated by Zhao Peng

Translated by Li Chaoyuan

Edited by Scott Huntsman

Published by Blossom Press

Address: No. 24 Baiwanzhuang Street, Xicheng District, Beijing 100037, China

Telephone: (8610) 68996522

Fax: (8610) 88415258 (Sales Department)

ISBN 978-7-5054-5343-2

Printed in the People's Republic of China